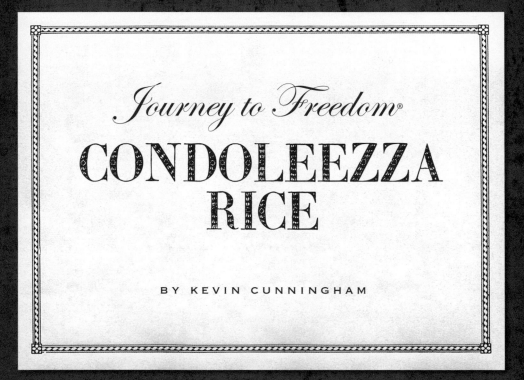

Journey to Freedom

CONDOLEEZZA RICE

BY KEVIN CUNNINGHAM

"I TELL MY STUDENTS, IF YOU FIND
YOURSELF IN THE COMPANY OF
PEOPLE WHO AGREE WITH YOU,
YOU'RE IN THE WRONG COMPANY."
— CONDOLEEZZA RICE

Cover and page 4:
Secretary of State Condoleezza
Rice at a function in Paris
in 2005

Content Consultant:
Glenn Kessler, diplomatic
correspondent, Washington
Post*; author,* The Confidante:
Condoleezza Rice and the
Creation of the Bush Legacy

Published in the United States of America by The Child's World®
1980 Lookout Drive, Mankato, MN 56003-1705
800-599-READ • www.childsworld.com

ACKNOWLEDGEMENTS

The Child's World®: Mary Berendes, Publishing Director

The Design Lab: Kathleen Petelinsek, Design and Page Production

Red Line Editorial: Holly Saari, Editorial Direction

PHOTOS

Cover and page 4: Horacio Villalobos/Corbis

Interior: AP Images: 7, 9, 23, 25; Barry Thumma/AP Images: 16; Bettmann/Corbis: 13; David
J. Phillip/AP Images: 21; Emilio Morenatti/AP Images: 26; Haraz N. Ghanbari/AP Images: 27;
Linda A. Cicero/AP Images: 15; Lionel Cironneau/AP Images: 17; Morton Beebe/Corbis: 14; Paul
Sakuma/AP Images: 20; Peter Turnley/Corbis: 19; Stillman College Archives: 10; University of
Denver Special Collections and Archives: 5, 11

LIBRARY OF CONGRESS CATALOGING-IN-PUBLICATION DATA

Cunningham, Kevin, 1966–

Condoleezza Rice / by Kevin Cunningham.

    p. cm. — (Journey to freedom)

Includes bibliographical references and index.

ISBN 978-1-60253-120-8 (library bound : alk. paper)

1. Rice, Condoleezza, 1954– 2. Stateswomen—United States—Biography—Juvenile literature.
3. Women cabinet officers—United States—Biography—Juvenile literature. 4. Cabinet officers—
United States—Biography—Juvenile literature. 5. African American women educators—Biography—Juvenile literature. 6. African American women—Biography—Juvenile literature. 7. African
Americans—Biography—Juvenile literature. I. Title.

E840.8.R48C86 2009

327.730092—dc22

[B]

2008031928

CONTENTS

Condoleezza Rice is the only child of two teachers. The Rices raised their daughter to value education.

Chapter One

DRIVEN TO SUCCEED

Right from the start, Condoleezza Rice achieved great things. As the only child of highly educated, motivated parents, she worked diligently to accomplish her many goals, despite facing obstacles such as **segregation** and **racism**. Whether it was mastering the piano, excelling in academics, or achieving one of the highest-ranking positions in the White House, Condoleezza Rice worked hard to make it happen.

Condoleezza was born in Birmingham, Alabama, on November 14, 1954. Her parents both had college educations and highly valued success and achievement in life. Condoleezza's father, John Wesley Rice Jr., was a guidance counselor and a Presbyterian minister. Her mother, Angelena Ray Rice, was a teacher who taught science, speech, and music to high school students.

Angelena took music very seriously. Condoleezza's mother, grandmother, and great-grandmother all played piano. Condoleezza's grandmother was also a piano teacher. At the age of three, Condoleezza began taking lessons from her. Condoleezza could read sheet music before she could read books.

The Rices were determined to educate their only child. Before beginning kindergarten, Condoleezza had studied French, ballet, and art in addition to being able to read and play piano.

Because Condoleezza could already read by the age of five, Angelena tried to put her in school. But the principal said she was too young. So Angelena took a year off from work to teach her daughter at home. In addition to schoolwork, Condoleezza continued piano lessons. Her mother also took her to museums to learn about art.

"I had parents who gave me every conceivable opportunity," Condoleezza Rice said years later. "They also believed in achievement."

When Condoleezza was growing up, Alabama and all of the southern states were segregated. Legal segregation involved laws that separated whites and blacks in many public places, including bathrooms, restaurants, movie theaters, and schools. These laws,

Angelena named Condoleezza for the Italian musical term con dolce **(kohn dohl-chay),** *which instructs a performer to play "with sweetness." She then experimented with e's and z's to come up with the name* Condoleezza.

called Jim Crow laws, were humiliating and unfair to blacks. For example, it was against the law for a black person to shake a white person's hand.

The Rices prepared Condoleezza for the reality of the Jim Crow laws in many ways. Condoleezza's parents taught her to be self-confident and proud and to not become upset when she would hear racist comments or see Jim Crow laws in action. When the Rices encountered racism, they demanded calmly and firmly to be treated as equals to whites. The Rices also made sure Condoleezza would be well-educated and successful. Birmingham's educated black community knew that its children would have to be twice as smart and twice as talented as white children to get respect. Condoleezza worked to be both.

But her childhood wasn't all work. Every Sunday, she and her father would sit on the couch and watch football games on television. John Rice, who was a former school coach and huge football fan, decided to teach the game to his daughter. Condoleezza's father explained the plays, the teams, and the rules to her. She developed a lifelong love of the game.

As a child, Condoleezza Rice lived in a segregated society. In the South, Jim Crow laws required black customers at this bus depot to wait in a separate room.

When Condoleezza finally started school, she was so far ahead that she skipped the first grade and later the seventh grade.

7

From an early age, Condoleezza showed a striking desire to learn. "Condoleezza's always been so focused, ever since she was really, really young," said her aunt, Genoa Ray McPhatter. "She would practice her piano at a certain time without anyone having to remind her." By the time Condoleezza was four, she had learned enough piano pieces to give her first performance.

As Condoleezza grew older, she became more aware of the conflict surrounding legal segregation. In the 1950s, the **civil rights movement** began. People in the movement began to protest against racist Jim Crow laws and to demand that those laws be thrown out. Many blacks and some whites banded together to fight for equal treatment, **integrated** schools, and fair voting opportunities.

By the early 1960s, the movement began to succeed. A number of whites in the South fought back with threats and violence. It was very unsafe. Bomb threats forced Condoleezza to miss many days of school. On September 15, 1963, a tragedy within the movement touched Condoleezza personally. During Sunday school at the Sixteenth Street Baptist Church, a bomb exploded. Four girls were killed, including one of Condoleezza's friends.

The civil rights movement marched ahead despite the violence. In 1964, President Lyndon Johnson signed the Civil Rights Act, ending legal segregation. A few days later, the Rices entered—and were served at—a formerly whites-only restaurant.

In 1969, John Rice earned his **master's degree**. Soon after, he got a job at the University of Denver and moved his family to Colorado. In Colorado, Condoleezza enrolled at St. Mary's Academy. It was the first integrated school she had attended. The students were smart and driven. Condoleezza's mature behavior, self-confidence, and intelligence impressed teachers.

The remains of the
Sixteenth Street
Baptist Church after
it was bombed on
September 15, 1963

Condoleezza Rice attends an event at Stillman College with her parents in 1967.

By the start of Condoleezza's senior year of high school, she already had enough credits to graduate. Her parents wanted her to start college. But in a rare moment of rebellion, she asked to finish high school with her friends. The Rices agreed, but only if Condoleezza started college part-time. So in addition to her high school classes, piano lessons, and ice-skating, she took college courses at the University of Denver.

Music continued to be important to her. After winning a piano contest, 15-year-old Condoleezza played with the Denver Symphony Orchestra. A career in music awaited her. But she surprised everyone, including herself, by turning onto a new path—one that would lead her to the White House.

At the University of Denver, Condoleezza Rice decided against a music career.

Chapter Two

A CHANGE OF PLANS

t the age of 16, Condoleezza Rice became a full-time student at the University of Denver. She studied piano until her second year in college. The following summer, she performed at a music festival in nearby Aspen, Colorado. There, she competed against students much more advanced than she was. While an excellent musician, Rice knew only the most brilliant became concert pianists. If she was only "pretty good but not great," as she said, she preferred to switch to a field where she could be great.

It was a difficult decision. Rice's parents had spent a lot of time and money training her for piano. Now she wanted to try studying something else. She didn't even know what to study. She tried government, but the classes bored her. She tried English literature, but she did not care for it.

One day in the spring of her third year of college, Rice heard a lecture on Joseph Stalin, the **dictator** of the Soviet Union. The Soviet Union was a large eastern European country that was following a form of government called **communism**. Rice was fascinated by what she heard. She decided to speak with the man giving the lecture, Dr. Josef Korbel.

Impressed with her intelligence, Korbel suggested Rice consider studying **international relations**. Korbel became her **mentor**. On his advice, she began to study Russian history and the Russian language. After that, she studied "Soviet politics, Soviet everything."

Though she came late to her new field of study, Rice worked hard and graduated with honors in 1974. After graduating, Rice headed east to the University of Notre Dame in Indiana to earn her master's degree. At Notre Dame, Rice studied about a major struggle for power called the **Cold War**.

At the end of World War II (1939–1945), much of the world separated into two groups: countries that believed in democracy and countries that followed communism. In democratic countries, such as the United States, citizens had the freedom to choose where to work, what to buy, and who their political leaders should be. In communist countries, such as the Soviet

Upon graduating from the University of Denver, Rice won an award for "outstanding accomplishment and promise in the field of political science." The school also named her Outstanding Senior Woman.

Workers at a government-run factory do morning exercises in Moscow, Soviet Union, in 1961.

Union, the people valued collective ownership. This was a system under which the citizens shared everything and everyone worked for the collective good.

Both the United States and the Soviet Union felt that their system of government was superior to the other. Because the two countries felt threatened by one another, the Cold War started. In the Cold War, neither side actually fought, but both sides had nuclear weapons that had the potential to destroy the other country.

Rice was very interested in the Cold War. At Notre Dame, she learned about how the Soviet Union used its military power. Her study of the Soviet military—its army, navy, and air force—would become a major part of her life.

As the year ended, Rice thought about going to law school. But Dr. Korbel changed her mind. "You are very talented," he said. "You have to become a professor." She had never considered that possibility. In August of 1975, 20-year-old Rice graduated with her master's degree. She then returned to the University of Denver and began work on her **doctorate**.

During the time that Rice was working on her doctorate, she became engaged to a member of the Denver Broncos football team. It was so serious that she began to sit with the other players' wives at games. The relationship ended, however. As with most things about her personal life, she has kept the details private.

After earning her doctorate, Condoleezza Rice moved to Palo Alto to teach political science at Stanford University.

While working on her doctorate, Rice interned for the U.S. Department of State in Washington DC. The internship gave her the chance to do research in the Soviet Union and see up close what she had read so much about at school.

Six years later, on August 14, 1981, Rice graduated with a doctorate in international studies. Soon after, she headed off to Palo Alto, California, to work as an assistant professor of political science at Stanford University.

Condoleezza Rice became a popular professor at Stanford University.

Chapter Three

A BOOMING CAREER

ondoleezza Rice enjoyed her teaching job at Stanford. Her energy, outgoing personality, and ability to back up strong opinions made her an ideal teacher. Soon, Rice became one of Stanford's most popular professors. In 1984, the university gave her its highest award for teaching.

In addition to her academic responsibilities, Rice worked for the Council on Foreign Relations in Washington DC. This group studied and reported on the United States' relationships with other countries, especially communist nations. Rice learned how the U.S. military worked, made decisions, and planned ahead. The experience proved to be invaluable.

President George H. W. Bush walks with his National Security Advisor Brent Scowcroft, who hired Condoleezza Rice to work with him.

Rice also had a very busy schedule outside of work. She did volunteer work in the community, served on several committees at Stanford University, and published two books on the Soviet Union.

Unfortunately, all of this work kept her away from her parents, who still lived in Denver. Angelena Rice became ill with breast cancer and died in 1985 at the age of 61. After the funeral service, Rice played some of her mother's favorite hymns on the piano as a tribute.

Meanwhile, the outside world was changing quickly. By the late 1980s, citizens in Eastern Europe were demanding reform, and the Soviet Union was ready to collapse. If it fell apart, the Cold War might finally end. No one knew what would happen. It was a confusing and dangerous time.

George H. W. Bush, the new president, needed experts on the Soviet Union. He had chosen a man named Brent Scowcroft to be the national security advisor. Scowcroft had met Rice at Stanford and remembered how knowledgeable she was on the Soviet Union. Now he needed her in Washington to provide her expertise during such a critical time.

On November 12, 1989, many East Germans flooded through the dismantled Berlin Wall into West Germany.

In 1989, Rice took over as director of Soviet and East European affairs on the U.S. National Security Council. That same year the Berlin Wall came down. Since its construction in 1961, the Berlin Wall had prevented the East Germans, who lived under communism, from moving to democratic West Germany. Soviet leader Mikhail Gorbachev asked for a meeting with U.S. officials to discuss reuniting East Germany and West Germany into one country again.

Rice sat at the table with Bush and Gorbachev. When the two men met, Bush introduced Rice, and said, "She tells me everything I know about the Soviet Union." Gorbachev, who was used to dealing with older white men, turned to Rice and promptly replied, "I hope you know a lot." As it turned out, Rice did know a lot, and she helped successfully negotiate bringing the two countries together.

In less than one year, Germany reunited. Less than a year after that, Russians voted for their own president. On Christmas Day in 1991, Gorbachev stepped down, and the Soviet Union—and the Cold War—soon came to an end.

With all of these changes in motion, Rice decided to return to Stanford University and continue her work as an associate professor. During this time, she also teamed up with her father and his second wife to start the Center for a New Generation. This after-school program trained promising students in language, performing arts, computers, math, and science. Rice wanted to provide the same kind of opportunities to children that her parents had provided for her so many years before. "Those are sort of my kids," she said of the children in the program. "All 125 of them."

By 1993, Rice was promoted to provost of Stanford University. As provost, she managed the university's

When Rice became provost at Stanford, the university had spent $20 million over its budget. Within two years, Rice managed to completely eliminate the deficit and even create a record budget surplus of more than $14 million for the university. However, not everyone at the university agreed with the budget cuts, or Rice's role as provost.

President George H. W. Bush and Soviet Leader Mikhail Gorbachev meet in 1990 at the White House to discuss unifying East and West Germany.

$1.5 billion budget and made decisions that affected the entire school. Not only was she the first woman and first black person to hold the job, but at the age of 38, she was also the youngest. The same year, Stanford made her a full professor. Soon, *Time* magazine declared her one of "50 Young Leaders to Watch." That prediction would soon prove to be true.

Over the years, Condoleezza Rice kept her ties with Stanford University. In 2002, she gave the commencement address at the university's graduation ceremonies.

During George W. Bush's first presidential campaign, Condoleezza Rice served as his chief foreign policy consultant. Here the two are with Paul Wolfowitz, another foreign policy advisor, at Bush's Texas Ranch.

Chapter Four

THE WHITE HOUSE AND BEYOND

ver the years, Rice had become close friends with the Bush family. So when George W. Bush, the former president's son, decided to run for president, Rice agreed to advise him on world affairs.

Bush was impressed with Rice's knowledge. Dealing with other countries is a big part of being president, and Bush had to be knowledgeable about various world problems. Rice and another advisor prepared Bush for the upcoming election by answering any questions he had on global issues. Sometimes they even talked while exercising or fishing.

When George W. Bush won the presidential election in 2000, he did not hesitate to appoint his advisor and close friend to the job of national security advisor. As national security advisor, Rice had the very important responsibility of formally counseling the president about U.S. security and foreign affairs. Rice was the first woman to hold this position.

Rice's father died just six days after she accepted the job. Although saddened, she prepared for her work at the White House. Soon, she would find herself playing very critical roles in many important world events.

On September 11, 2001, terrorists hijacked four planes and attacked the World Trade Center in New York City and the Pentagon in Washington DC. Rice immediately called her aunt and uncle in Birmingham, Alabama, told them she was safe, and got to work.

Soon an investigation pegged the hijackers as members of al-Qaeda, a terrorist organization. Plans had to be made about how to respond.

When the president decided to attack al-Qaeda in its main hiding place, Afghanistan, Rice was part of the team that created the Bush Doctrine. This policy declared the United States would fight terrorist organizations, such as al-Qaeda, as well as countries that hid or helped these organizations.

The United States defeated Afghanistan's government in five weeks. President Bush and his advisors turned their attention to another country that

On September 12, 2001, President Bush met with his National Security Council, including National Security Advisor Condoleezza Rice, to plan a response to the September 11 terrorist attack.

they believed helped terrorists—Iraq. For a time, various people in government disagreed about what to do. Some wanted war. Others preferred to work with the United Nations to apply pressure on Iraq.

Rice believed Iraq's dictator, Saddam Hussein, was dangerous. When President Bush decided to go to war, Rice explained why the United States needed to attack. One of the main dangers, she said, was that Hussein might have chemical, biological, or nuclear weapons.

Rice made her feelings very clear in August of 2003, after Hussein had been defeated. "Saddam Hussein's regime posed a threat to the security of the United States and the world. That threat could not be allowed to remain unaddressed," Rice said.

As the war continued, however, Rice faced criticism when no weapons of mass destruction (WMDs) could be found in Iraq. She did not back down. She responded to the criticism by stating that the invasion of Iraq had still been needed as a means to stop Saddam Hussein from developing WMDs.

In 2004, President Bush was elected for a second term as president. After his re-election, Bush asked Rice to become the new U.S. secretary of state, the country's top diplomat.

As U.S. secretary of state, Rice continued to help the president on issues relating to foreign affairs. Rice visited other countries—sometimes several within a single day—and spoke with other nations'

President Bush has a deep respect and admiration for Condoleezza Rice. When Bush nominated Rice for secretary of state, he remarked that, "Above all, Dr. Rice has a deep, abiding belief in the value and power of liberty, because she has seen freedom denied and freedom reborn."

In 2005, Condoleezza Rice was sworn in as secretary of state, one of the highest-ranking positions in the White House.

representatives on issues ranging from trade in South America to nuclear weapons in North Korea.

One of the major issues on which Rice had focused much of her time involved the ongoing conflict between the Israeli and Palestinian territories. Since Israel was established in 1948, the two groups have fought over valued land within the region.

In an effort to achieve a peaceful resolution, Rice made many trips to the region and even managed to coordinate several meetings between Israeli Prime Minister Ehud Olmert and Palestinian President Mahmoud Abbas.

Much of Rice's work as U.S. secretary of state was put toward what she called "transformational

Condoleezza Rice shakes hands with Palestinian President Mahmoud Abbas in 2007. Working toward a peaceful resolution of the Israeli-Palestinian conflict has been a top priority for her.

diplomacy." Transformational diplomacy involved encouraging nations to have democratic, self-sustaining governments that would be able to work well in an international political structure.

Although some critics felt that Rice and the United States government were becoming overly involved in the internal affairs of other countries, Rice remained optimistic. "I watched the president standing in front of an American and Afghan flag, and I thought, the American president can now stand in front of an American and Iraqi flag, an American and Lebanese flag, and an American and Palestinian flag. I think in six years to have helped to foster those changes, even if they're incomplete, even if they're tough, even if there's still work to be done. . . . Those are pretty dramatic changes."

As President Bush's second term in office came to an end, Rice continued to be an influential and leading figure. In the future, she should have many more opportunities to make an impact on history.

Condoleezza Rice prepares to speak at the groundbreaking ceremony for the George P. Shultz National Foreign Affairs Training Center in 2007.

Time Line

1954
On November 14, Condoleezza Rice is born to John and Angelena Rice in Birmingham, Alabama.

1963
On September 15, a bomb set by the Ku Klux Klan explodes at Birmingham's Sixteenth Street Baptist Church. Four girls, including an 11-year-old friend of Condoleezza's, die in the blast.

1965
Condoleezza enters the Birmingham Southern Conservatory of Music to study piano, flute, and violin.

1969
John Rice gets a job at the University of Denver. The Rice family moves to Denver, where Condoleezza attends an integrated school for the first time.

1974
Rice graduates with honors from the University of Denver at the age of 19.

1975
Rice earns her master's degree in government from the University of Notre Dame.

1977
Rice works as an intern with the U.S. Department of State.

1981
Rice earns her doctorate from the Graduate School of International Studies at the University of Denver.

1984
Rice wins Stanford University's highest award for teaching. That same year, she publishes her first book, *Uncertain Allegiance: The Soviet Union and the Czechoslovak Army, 1948–1963.*

1986
Rice (with Alexander Dallin) publishes her second book, *The Gorbachev Era.*

1987
Rice becomes an associate professor of political science at Stanford University.

1989
Rice takes over as director of Soviet and East European Affairs on the National Security Council. Later, she is promoted to senior director.

1990
Rice sits at the bargaining table during the meetings between U.S. president George H. W. Bush and Soviet leader Mikhail Gorbachev. Later, she serves as presidential advisor during Gorbachev's visit to Washington DC.

1991
Rice returns to Stanford as an associate professor.

1993
Rice becomes a full professor and accepts the position of provost at Stanford University. She is the first woman and the first black person to hold the job. She serves until 1999.

1995
Rice (with Philip Zelikow) publishes the book, *Germany Unified and Europe Transformed: A Study in Statecraft.*

1999
Rice advises Texas governor and Republican presidential candidate George W. Bush on foreign policy.

2000
On December 18, Rice is named national security advisor. Six days later, her father dies.

2001
Rice is sworn in as national security advisor.

2002
Rice receives the NAACP (National Association for the Advancement of Colored People) President's Award for leadership in promoting the advancement of minorities.

2003
Rice receives an honorary degree from the Mississippi College School of Law.

2004
President George W. Bush nominates Rice for secretary of state.

GLOSSARY

civil rights movement
(*siv*-il rites **moov**-munt)
The civil rights movement is the name given to the struggle for equal rights for blacks in the United States during the 1950s and 1960s. Rice witnessed the civil rights movement when she was growing up.

Cold War
(**kohld wor**)
The Cold War was the struggle for world power between the United States and the Soviet Union that lasted from 1945 to 1991, when the Soviet Union collapsed. Rice studied the Soviet Union and the Cold War.

communism
(**kom**-yuh-niz-uhm)
Communism is a form of government that allows for all land, businesses, and profits to be shared by the government or community. Rice learned about communism during her studies of the Soviet Union.

dictator
(**dik**-tay-tur)
A dictator is the sole ruler of a country who often rules unfairly. Joseph Stalin was dictator of the Soviet Union from 1929 to 1953.

doctorate
(**dok**-tur-uht)
A doctorate is the most advanced educational degree. Rice earned a doctorate in international studies.

integrated
(**in**-tuh-gray-tuhd)
Different things combined together into one group are integrated. St. Mary's Academy was the first integrated school Rice attended.

international relations
(in-tur-**nash**-uh-nuhl ri-**lay**-shunz)
International relations is the branch of politics that focuses on relationships between countries. Rice is an expert in the field of international relations.

master's degree
(**mass**-turs di-**gree**)
A master's degree is the educational degree that comes after a bachelor's degree. Rice earned a master's degree from Notre Dame.

mentor
(**men**-tur)
A mentor is both a role model and a teacher. Josef Korbel was Rice's mentor.

racism
(**ray**-sih-zum)
Racism is the belief that one race is superior to another. When the Rice family encountered racism, they demanded to be treated as equals to whites.

segregation
(seg-ruh-**gay**-shun)
Segregation is the act of keeping race, class, or ethnic groups apart. For part of Condoleezza's childhood, segregation kept whites and blacks separate in schools and public facilities.

Further Information

Books

Grant, Reg G. *Cold War*. London: Arcturus, 2007.

Hughes, Karen. *George W. Bush: Portrait of a Leader*. Wheaton, IL: Tyndale, 2005.

McNeese, Tim. *Civil Rights Movement: Striving for Justice*. New York: Chelsea House, 2007.

Morrison, Toni. *Remember: The Journey to School Integration*. New York: Houghton Mifflin, 2004.

Rinaldo, Denise. *White House*. New York: HarperCollins, 2008.

Ruffin, David C. *Duties and Responsibilities of the Secretary of State*. New York: Rosen Publishing, 2005.

Videos

Biography: Condoleezza Rice. A&E Networks, 2005.

A History of Black Achievement in America. Dir. Scott Gordon. Ambrose, 2005.

Web Sites

Visit our Web page for links about Condoleezza Rice:

http://www.childsworld.com/links

NOTE TO PARENTS, TEACHERS, AND LIBRARIANS: We routinely verify our Web links to make sure they are safe, active sites—so encourage your readers to check them out!

Index